Sleeping
with the
Dictionary

NEW CALIFORNIA POETRY

EDITED BY | Robert Hass
Calvin Bedient
Brenda Hillman

For, by Carol Snow
Enola Gay, by Mark Levine
Selected Poems, by Fanny Howe
Sleeping with the Dictionary, by Harryette Mullen
Commons, by Myung Mi Kim
The Guns and Flags Project, by Geoffrey G. O'Brien

Harryette Mullen

Sleeping
with the Dictionary

University of California Press

Berkeley   Los Angeles   London

University of California Press
Berkeley and Los Angeles, California

University of California Press, Ltd.
London, England

© 2002 by the Regents of the
University of California

Library of Congress Cataloging-in-
Publication Data
Mullen, Harryette Romell.
  Sleeping with the dictionary /
Harryette Mullen.
      p.   cm.—(New California
poetry ; 4)
ISBN 0-520-23143-0 (pbk. alk. paper)
    1. Language and languages—Poetry.
    2. African Americans—Poetry.
I. Title. II. Series.

PS3563.U3954 S64   2002
811'.54—dc21   2001048050

Printed in Canada
11 10 09 08 07 06 05 04 03
10 9 8 7 6 5 4 3

The paper used in this publication
meets the minimum requirements of
ANSI/NISO Z39.48-1992 (R 1997)
(*Permanence of Paper*). ♾

Dark words
more radiant
than onyx!

André Breton

Contents

Acknowledgments

I gratefully acknowledge the editors of the following publications and web projects, where these poems have previously appeared: *African American Review, A Gathering of the Tribes, American Poet, Aufgabe, Best American Poetry, Black Renaissance, Bombay Gin, Booglite, Callaloo, Cave Canem Anthology, Colored Greens, Columbia Poetry Review, Combo, Crow, Dia Center for the Arts Poetry Broadside, Empty Set, Facture, Fence, Framework, Gare du Nord, Giant Steps, Hambone, In Celebration of the Muse, Konch, La Jornada Semanal, La Vitrina, Lipstick Eleven, Long News in the Short Century, Mirage, Otra Canción: Seis Poetas Norteamericanos, Parnassus, Poetry in Motion, Role Call, Santa Monica Review, Southfields, The World, Tripwire, Womenhouse,* and *Xcp: Cross Cultural Poetics.*

My thanks to Enrique Chagoya for permission to use his work *Line Essence Color* on the cover. Thanks also to Judy Natal for the author photograph.

Sleeping
with the
Dictionary

Forgive me, I'm no good at this. I can't write back. I never read your letter. I can't say I got your note. I haven't had the strength to open the envelope. The mail stacks up by the door. Your hand's illegible. Your postcards were defaced. "Wash your wet hair"? Any document you meant to send has yet to reach me. The untied parcel service never delivered. I regret to say I'm unable to reply to your unexpressed desires. I didn't get the book you sent. By the way, my computer was stolen. Now I'm unable to process words. I suffer from aphasia. I've just returned from Kenya and Korea. Didn't you get a card from me yet? What can I tell you? I forgot what I was going to say. I still can't find a pen that works and then I broke my pencil. You know how scarce paper is these days. I admit I haven't been recycling. I never have time to read the *Times*. I'm out of shop-ping bags to put the old news in. I didn't get to the market. I meant to clip the coupons. I haven't read the mail yet. I can't get out the door to work, so I called in sick. I went to bed with writer's cramp. If I couldn't get back to writing, I thought I'd catch up on my reading. Then *Oprah* came on with a fabulous author plugging her best-selling book.

The Anthropic Principle

The pope of cosmology addresses a convention. When he talks
the whole atmosphere changes. He speaks through a computer.
When he asks can you hear me, the whole audience says yes. It's
a science locked up in a philosophical debate. There are a few
different theories. There could be many different realities. You
might say ours exists because we do. You could take a few
pounds of matter, heat it to an ungodly temperature, or the uni-
verse was a freak accident. There may be a limit to our arro-
gance, but one day the laws of physics will read like a detailed
instruction manual. A plane that took off from its hub in my
hometown just crashed in the President's hometown. The news
anchor says the pilot is among the dead. I was hoping for news
of the President's foreign affair with a diplomat's wife. I felt a
mystical connection to the number of confirmed dead whose
names were not released. Like the time I was three handshakes
from the President. Like when I thought I heard that humani-
tarians dropped a smart blond on the Chinese embassy. Like
when the cable was severed and chairs fell from the sky because
the pilot flew with rusty maps. What sane pilot would land in
that severe rain with hard hail and gale-force wind. With no
signal of distress. With no foghorns to warn the civilians, the

pilot lost our moral compass in the bloody quagmire of collateral damage. One theory says it's just a freak accident locked up in a philosophical debate. It's like playing poker and all the cards are wild. Like the arcane analysis of a black box full of insinuations of error.

You are a ukulele beyond my microphone

You are a Yukon beyond my Micronesia

You are a union beyond my meiosis

You are a unicycle beyond my migration

You are a universe beyond my mitochondria

You are a Eucharist beyond my Miles Davis

You are a euphony beyond my myocardiogram

You are a unicorn beyond my Minotaur

You are a eureka beyond my maitai

You are a Yuletide beyond my minesweeper

You are a euphemism beyond my myna bird

You are a unit beyond my mileage

You are a Yugoslavia beyond my mind's eye

You are a yoo-hoo beyond my minor key

You are a Euripides beyond my mime troupe

You are a Utah beyond my microcosm

You are a Uranus beyond my Miami

You are a youth beyond my mylar

You are a euphoria beyond my myalgia

You are a Ukrainian beyond my Maimonides

You are a Euclid beyond my miter box

You are a Univac beyond my minus sign

You are a Eurydice beyond my maestro

You are a eugenics beyond my Mayan

You are a U-boat beyond my mind control
You are a euthanasia beyond my miasma
You are a urethra beyond my Mysore
You are a Euterpe beyond my Mighty Sparrow
You are a ubiquity beyond my minority
You are a eunuch beyond my migraine
You are a Eurodollar beyond my miserliness
You are a urinal beyond my Midol
You are a uselessness beyond my myopia

Ask Aden

for A. D.

Are aardvarks anxious?

Do dragons dream?

Ever see an eager elephant?

Newts are never nervous, are they?

My ass acts bad
Devil your ears Charybdis
Good engagements deep blue sea
Heaven my eyes your elbow
Last night jobs hard place
Now his legs hell
Rock the lines me
Scylla her breasts shinola
Shit the sheets then
Yesterday my thighs this morning
You your toes today

Californians say No
to bilingual instruction in schools

Californians say No
to bilingual instructions on ballots

Californians say Yes
to bilingual instructions on curbside waste receptacles:

Coloque el recipiente con las flechas hacia la calle
Place container with arrow facing street

No ruede el recipiente con la tapa abierta
Do not tilt or roll container with lid open

Recortes de jardin solamente
Yard clippings only

We need quarters like King Tut needed a boat. A slave could row him to heaven from his crypt in Egypt full of loot. We've lived quietly among the stars, knowing money isn't what matters. We only bring enough to tip the shuttle driver when we hitch a ride aboard a trailblazer of light. This comet could scour the planet. Make it sparkle like a fresh toilet swirling with blue. Or only come close enough to brush a few lost souls. Time is rotting as our bodies wait for now I lay me down to earth. Noiseless patient spiders paid with dirt when what we want is stardust. If nature abhors an expensive appliance, why does the planet suck ozone? This is a big-ticket item, a thickety ride. Please page our home and visit our sigh on the wide world's ebb. Just point and cluck at our new persuasion shoes. We're opening the gate that opens our containers for recycling. Time to throw down and take off on our launch. This flight will nail our proof of pudding. The thrill of victory is, we're exiting earth. We're leaving all this dirt.

•

Ack-ack, aye-aye.

Baa baa, Baba, Bambam, Bebe, Berber, Bibi, blah-blah, Bobo, bonbon,

booboo, Bora Bora, Boutros Boutros, bye-bye.

Caca, cancan, Cece, cha-cha, chichi, choo-choo, chop chop, chow chow, Coco, cocoa,

come come, cuckoo.

Dada, Dee Dee, Didi, dindin, dodo, doodoo, dumdum, Duran Duran.

Fifi, fifty-fifty, foofoo, froufrou.

Gaga, Gigi, glug-glug, go-go, goody-goody, googoo, grisgris.

Haha, harhar, hear hear, heehee, hey hey, hip-hip, hoho, Hsing-Hsing, hubba-hubba, humhum.

is is, It'sIts.

JarJar, Jo Jo, juju.

Kiki, knock knock, Koko, Kumkum.

Lala, Lili, Ling-Ling looky-looky, Lulu.

Mahi mahi, mama, Mau Mau, Mei-Mei, Mimi, Momo, murmur, my my.

Na Na, No-no, now now.

Oh-oh, oink oink.

Pago Pago, Palau Palau, papa, pawpaw, peepee, Phen Fen, pooh-pooh, poopoo, pupu, putt-putt.

Rah-rah, ReRe.

Shih-Shih, Sing Sing, Sirhan Sirhan, Sen Sen, Sisi, so-so.

Tata, taki-taki, talky-talky, Tam Tam, Tartar, teetee, Tintin, Tingi Tingi, tom-tom, toot toot, tsetse, tsk tsk, tutu, tumtum, tut tut.

Van Van, veve, vroom-vroom.

Wahwah, Walla Walla, weewee, win-win.

Yadda yadda Yari Yari, yaya, ylang ylang, yo-yo, yuk-yuk, yum-yum.

Zizi, ZsaZsa, Zouzou, Zuzu.

Crenshaw is a juicy melon. Don't spit, and when you're finished, wash your neck. Tonight we lead with bleeding hearts, sliced raw or scooped with a spoon. I'll show my shank. I'd rend your cares with my shears. If I can't scare cash from the ashen crew, this monkey wrench has scratch to back my business. This ramshackle stack of shotguns I'm holding in my scope. I'm beady-eyed as a bug. Slippery as a sardine. Salty as a kipper. You could rehash me for breakfast. Find my shrinking awe, or share your wink. I'll get a rash wench. We'll crash a shower of cranes. I'm making bird seed to stick in a hen's craw. Where I live's a wren shack. Pull back. Show wreck. Black fade.

Bolsa Algodón

A sack lined with silver
Coin purse full of change
Able windbag puckered to blow kisses
Plump white pillows on blue coverlet
Some Dixie gents bowling
In a giant football stadium
Shake a sack lined with silver
Coin purse full of change

Watching television in Los Angeles. This scene performed in real time. In real life, a pretty picture walking and sitting still. It's still life with fried spam, lite poundcake, nondairy creme. It's death by chocolate. It's corporate warfare as we know it. I'm stuck on the fourth step. There's no statue or stature of limitations. I'll be emotionally disturbed for as long as it takes. You can give a man a rock or you can teach him to rock. Access your higher power. Fax back the map of your spiritual path. Take twenty drops tincture of worry wort. Who's paying for this if you're not covered? You're too simple to be so difficult. Malicious postmodernism. Petroleum jelly donut dunked in elbow grease. You look better going than coming. You look like death eating microwave popcorn. Now that I live alone, I'm much less introspective. Now you sound more like yourself.

da red
yell ow
bro won t
an orange you
bay jaun
pure people
blew hue
a gree gree in
viol let
purepeople
be lack
why it
pee ink

More than a woman's name. Her traditional shape. Rapidly
spread and rubbed with a wedge. Straight drunk with a crooked
lick. A brief suck on time. Diminutive. Promptly popular still
on the border. As one version of stamina went. A great show of
suffering in order to arouse. There were sweet ones. Frozen
ones and fruity ones. Her little resemblance to the original.
Shake her one key part. Control her ice. Shake her poor stem.
Her rim rubbed. Slice juice and pour control out with dusty salt.
Or to taste if desired.

Denigration

Did we surprise our teachers who had niggling doubts about the picayune brains of small black children who reminded them of clean pickaninnies on a box of laundry soap? How muddy is the Mississippi compared to the third-longest river of the darkest continent? In the land of the Ibo, the Hausa, and the Yoruba, what is the price per barrel of nigrescence? Though slaves, who were wealth, survived on niggardly provisions, should inheritors of wealth fault the poor enigma for lacking a dictionary? Does the mayor demand a recount of every bullet or does city hall simply neglect the black alderman's district? If I disagree with your beliefs, do you chalk it up to my negligible powers of discrimination, supposing I'm just trifling and not worth considering? Does my niggling concern with trivial matters negate my ability to negotiate in good faith? Though Maroons, who were unruly Africans, not loose horses or lazy sailors, were called renegades in Spanish, will I turn any blacker if I renege on this deal?

Dim Lady

My honeybunch's peepers are nothing like neon. Today's special at Red Lobster is redder than her kisser. If Liquid Paper is white, her racks are institutional beige. If her mop were Slinkys, dishwater Slinkys would grow on her noggin. I have seen tablecloths in Shakey's Pizza Parlors, red and white, but no such picnic colors do I see in her mug. And in some minty-fresh mouthwashes there is more sweetness than in the garlic breeze my main squeeze wheezes. I love to hear her rap, yet I'm aware that Muzak has a hipper beat. I don't know any Marilyn Monroes. My ball and chain is plain from head to toe. And yet, by gosh, my scrumptious Twinkie has as much sex appeal for me as any lanky model or platinum movie idol who's hyped beyond belief.

Dream Cycle

The ice cream truck
    goes by again

It could snow me
    under this heat

It could freeze my teeth
    crystallize a sigh

    and I could lick
    a quick dream

    when the ice cream truck
    goes lullaby again

A stout bomb wrapped with a bow. With wear, you tear. It's true you sour or rust. Some of us were sure you're in a rut. We bore your somber rub and storm. You were true, but you rust. On our tour out, we tore, we two. You were to trust in us, and we in you. Terribly, you tear. You tear us. You tell us you're true. Are you sure? Most of you bow to the mob. Strut with worms, strew your woe. So store your tears, tout your worst. Be a brute, if you must. You tear us most terribly. To the tomb, we rue our rust and rot. You tear. You wear us out. You try your best, but we're bust. You tear out of us. We tear from stem to stem. You trouble, you butter me most. You tear, but you tell us, trust us to suture you.

They just can't seem to . . . They should try harder to . . . They ought to be more . . . We all wish they weren't so . . . They never . . . They always . . . Sometimes they . . . Once in a while they . . . However it is obvious that they . . . Their overall tendency has been . . . The consequences of which have been . . . They don't appear to understand that . . . If only they would make an effort to . . . But we know how difficult it is for them to . . . Many of them remain unaware of . . . Some who should know better simply refuse to . . . Of course, their perspective has been limited by . . . On the other hand, they obviously feel entitled to . . . Certainly we can't forget that they . . . Nor can it be denied that they . . . We know that this has had an enormous impact on their . . . Nevertheless their behavior strikes us as . . . Our interactions unfortunately have been . . .

European Folk Tale Variant

for the archives of Toni Cade Bambara

The way the story goes, a trespassing towheaded pre-teen barged into the rustic country cottage of a nuclear family of anthropomorphic bruins. Her motivation? Who can be sure? Some say the youthful offender was an innocent maiden who lost her sense of direction in the lush growth of the virgin pine forest. Or perhaps the elders of her tribe had neglected to attend to her proper socialization. In any case, this flaxen-haired vixen perpetrated a "B and E," a felony punishable by law. The incorrigible pre-adolescent didn't stop with trespassing, or even with breaking and entering. The finicky home invader helped herself to generous portions of the ursine honey eaters' whole grain breakfast cereal, vandalized their heirloom antique furniture. Then, after tiring herself out with so much wanton destruction, the platinum blonde delinquent took a refreshing beauty nap in the bruin family's bedroom—just like she thought she was a guest at a cozy bed and breakfast inn. Returning from their fishing expedition, the family could barely express their shock and dismay, seeing the shambles the puerile hoodlum had made of their woodland homestead. Despite their emotional trauma, they successfully expelled the rude intruder from their charming bungalow. With the assistance of the neighborhood crime patrol, law enforcement officers were able to apprehend and incarcerate the callow miscreant, who has been sentenced to juvenile detention. Attorneys representing the Ursidae family interests have filed suit against the criminally negligent parents of the wayward youth, and expect that the bruins will be awarded a substantial sum for emotional distress as well as for extensive damage to their property.

Can't wait to be sprung from shadow,
to be known from a hole in the ground.
Scarcely silent though often unheard.
Winding, wound. Wounded wind.
She turned, and turns. She opens.
Keep the keys, that devil told her.
Guess the question. Dream the answer.
Tore down almost level.
A silence hardly likely.
Juicy voices. Pour them on.
Music sways her, she concedes,
as darker she goes deeper.

Exploring the Dark Content

This dream is not a map.
A poem is not the territory.

The dreamer reclines in a barbershop
carpeted with Afro turf.
In the dark some soul yells.

It hurts to walk barefoot
on cowrie shells.

Fancy Cortex

reading Jayne Cortez

I'm using my plain brain to imagine her fancy cortex. As if my lowly mollusk could wear so exalted a mantle as her pontifex pallium. As if the knots and tangles of my twisted psyche could mesh with her intricate synaptic network of condensed neural convolutions. As if my simple chalk could fossilize the memory of her monumental reefs of caulifloral coral. As if my shallow unschooled shoals could reckon the calculus of her konk's brainwave tsunami. As if the pedestrian software of my mundane explorer could map as rounded colonies the *terra incognita* of her undiscovered hemispheres. As if the speculative diagnosis of my imaging technology could chart the direction of her intuitive intellect. As if the inquisitive iris of my galaxy-orbiting telescope could see as far as her vision. As if the trained nostrils of my narco-bloodhound could sniff out what she senses in the wind. As if my duty-free bottle of jerk sauce could simulate the fire ant *picante* that inflames her tongue of rage. As if the gray matter of my dim bulb could be enlightened by the brilliance of her burning watts. As if her divergent universification might fancy the microcosm of my prosaic mind.

She brought the radish for the horses, but not a bouquet for Mother's Day. She brought the salad to order with an unleavened joke. Let us dive in and turn up green in search of our roots. She sang the union maid with a lefty longshoreman. They all sang rusty freedom songs, once so many tongues were loosened. She went to bed sober as always, without a drop of wine. She was invited to judge a spectacle. They were a prickly pair in a restaurant of two-way mirrors with rooms for interrogation. The waiter who brought a flaming dessert turned the heat from bickering to banter. She braked for jerk chicken on her way to meet the patron saint of liposuction. His face was cut from the sunflower scene, as he was stuffing it with cheesecake. Meanwhile, she slurped her soup alone at the counter before the gig. Browsers can picture his uncensored bagel rolling around in cyberspace. His half-baked metaphor with her scrambled ego. They make examples of intellectuals who don't appreciate property. She can't just trash the family-style menu or order by icon. Now she's making *kimchee* for the museum that preserved her history in a jar of pickled pig feet. They'd fix her oral tradition or she'd trade her oral fixation. Geechees are rice eaters. It's good to get a rice cooker if you cook a lot of rice. Please steam these shellfish at your own risk. Your mother eats blue-green algae to rid the body of free radicals.

He wants to know if I am happy here and have I eaten any apples yet. I tell him no, I like to let them fall off the trees and rot. They won't turn red and the ones I like to eat are red, but these sweeten the air with their decay. They are eaten. They are never wasted. They have their use, when they fall, never far from proverbial tree. Yellow apples falling with brown leaves more slowly onto grass that's greener than ever. Green in winter, tawny in summer. Don't burn. Consume yourself more slowly.

Right now the ground is damp and marshy. In summer there were many fires. Some started maliciously, others were spontaneous. Apple trees are here but he's not sure they belong. He dreams of rice growing where they are, a hilarious dream. The blood of agrarian ancestors does him no good. Some of his favorite trees are books. Besides, if he grew rice, which anyone knows he'd never do, where would the squirrels live? The black one was the aggressor, chasing tail. She flicked her tail in his face.

Squirrels multiply on his tree-filled acres. The sky is clear blue. A cloudless sky with two airplanes flying at different angles. Each is given a line, a path to fly in. The pilots communicate with someone on the ground. They all communicate with precise machines that very rarely make a fatal error. The ground is damp and moldy and a fire not likely to start in the air this time of year. Spontaneous combustion, midair collision. Try not to burn. Try not to alarm. The phone rang but she didn't answer it. Later he will ask her where she went and she will say, "To the laundromat or the library, I forget which." He might seem hurt but his honesty will prevail and he'll become earnest and blunt. That's when he starts to smoke. He'll want to get to the bottom of it, clear the air, work it through. At times like these he's most endearing and yet she'll have no place to hide because the house has no walls.

He can see her from another room. He likes to whisper at her while a record is playing. That's how cool he can be. He'll ask which books she's been reading. She could give him a list and we could discuss them later. We could gossip about books, which was one of his favorite activities. He didn't want to forbid her singing in the bathtub, but she would notice that he flinched a little, so she tried not to do it when he was around. She had not inherited the gene for music, just as his blood had distinguished itself from the red stuff of his ancestors. At all times he tried to indulge her, having heard the story of her austere childhood. She in turn would try to soothe and distract him from the score of abandonments that caused him such pain when remembered. They both had violent histories but longed to live in peace and so it was a pact sealed in blood, a sweetheart contract in which there were provisions for each to get the upper hand. Even though she bled every month, she always had someone to blame; while he noted that each time he touched her, her body was there, which had not always been the case with her predecessors.

She listened to his lists and made her own in secret. A grocery list was necessary because he avoided buying food, preferring to spend cash on inessentials because they bought more satisfaction. "But you," he told her, "are impossible to satisfy because you never seem to want, except to sleep and eat." She lives in his house like a sleepy cat though once he joked he might pay to keep her here, because even a woman with no wants must have money to supply her needs.

He never seems to sleep or eat but lives on a mysterious energy source, adapted for life on her planet. That's why she can't laugh at his jokes, because humor is local. He was born far away but feels at home. Or he was born close to home but feels far from there now. Nothing touches him now except her hands, her mouth. He touches her hair. Her wet hair. He makes her a gift of his solitude. Solitude is something she misses. He takes hers with him when he leaves. She goes out for short walks, looking at sidewalks. He takes her to mountains and deserts. He seeks out old trees. They walk until she's out of breath. "Chill," he says, and she feels cold, suddenly noticing the air.

Quantum mechanics fixed my karma wagon
Gypsies want to hold my hand
Dr. Duck recommends
      soap and ream therapies
With remedies like these
   who needs friends?

ab flab abracadabra Achy Breaky Action Jackson airy-fairy
airfare
Asian contagion analysis paralysis Anna banana
ants in your pants
Annie's Cranny Annie Fanny A-Okay ape drape argle-bargle
artsy-fartsy awesome blossom

backpack backtrack Bahama Mama balls to the wall bam-a-lam
bandstand
Battle in Seattle beat the meat bedspread bee's knees
behani ghani best dressed
best in the West BestRest Best Western Betsy Wetsy
Better Cheddar Big Dig bigwig
bird turd black don't crack blackjack blame game boho
boiling oil
Bone Phone Bonton Bony Maroni boob tube boogie-woogie
boohoo book nook
boon coon Bot's dots Boozy Suzy bowl of soul bow-wow
boy toy brace face
brain drain bric-a-brac bug jug bump on the rump
Busty Rusty

cachi-bachi caffe latte cake bake candy's dandy Care Bear
cash for trash Cat in the Hat

chalk talk Chatty Cathy cheers & jeers cheaper to keep her
cheat sheet Chester the molester
chewy gooey chick flick Chilly Willy chips & dips chitchat
chock-a-block
Choco Taco chop shop chrome dome Chubby Hubby
Chuck & Buck chugalug Chunky Monkey
cigar bar Cinni Mini claptrap Click & Clack clink-clank
clipclop Coca-Cola cock block
cock doc cock sock cookbook Cool Yule Cracker Jack
crack shack crack's wack creature feature
crick-crack crinkly wrinkly crisscross crop top crumb bum
Crunch 'n Munch
culture vulture curly-whirly

date rape deadhead deep sleep dikes on bikes dilly-dally
ding-a-ling ding-dang dingle-dangle
ding-dong dirty birdy Dizzy Lizzy dog log Don Juan
Donut Hut double trouble downtown dramarama
drape shape dream team Dress for Success drill & kill
drip-drop drunk skunk dry eye

eager beaver Earl the Pearl easy greasy Eat a Pita
eenie-meenie Etch-a-Sketch
Evel Knievel Even Stephen Eye in the Sky

fag hag fair share Fakin' Bacon fancy pants Fast Gas fat cat
  Fax Pax Fay Wray
fender bender fews & twos fiddle-faddle fight or flight Fiji
  file or pile fill the bill fine line
finer diner fine wine Flavor Saver Fleet Street flim-flam
  flip-flop Flirty Gerty Flo Jo
flower power flub-dub fly-by fly-by-night fly guy fogdog
  four-door four-on-the-floor
Foxy Roxy frat rat Freaks & Geeks freaky-deaky free bee
  frick & frack
fried, dyed, laid to the side fright night Froot Loops FuBu
  fuck a duck fuddyduddy
fungus among us fun in the sun funny money fur burger
  fuzzy wuzzy

gal pal gang bang gas grass or ass gator bait gay for pay
  Geechee gender bender
Georgie Porgie gewgaw gherkin jerkin gibber-jabber glad pad
  gloom & doom goof proof
googly-moogly Gorgeous George gory story Greeks & geeks
  Greek Week green bean
Green Jeans grinning & skinning

Hackensack hackmatack hackysack hair care hairy fairy
  Handy Andy
handy dandy hanky-panky hari-kari Happy to Be Nappy
  harum-scarum
haunch & paunch haste makes waste heart smart
  Heckle & Jeckle heebie-jeebies
Hegel's Bagels hell's bells helter-skelter Henny Penny
  herky-jerky heyday hickory-dickory
hi-fi higgledy-piggledy high & dry hinky dinky hip hop
  hippy dippy hobnob hobo
Hobson-Jobson hockey jockey hocus-pocus hodgepodge
  hoi polloi hoity-toity
HoJo Hokey Pokey holy mole holy moley Home Alone
  honey bunny Hong Kong honky-tonk
hoodoo hooked on books hook or crook hootchie-kootchie
  hotch-potch Hotel No Tell hot pot
hot shot Hottentot How now brown cow hubbub
  Hubba Bubba hubble-bubble Huckabuck
huff & puff hugger mugger Huey, Dewey, Louie Hully Gully
  humdrum hump & dump
Humpty-Dumpty hurdy-gurdy hurly-burly Hurry Curry
  hurry-scurry hustle & bustle

Icky Ricky I Like Ike ill pill ill will Increase the Peace
  inky-dinky
ism jism I Spy itsy-bitsy itty-bitty

jai alai Janet's Planet jeepers creepers Jeez Louise jelly belly
  jet set Jew canoe jig rig jimjams
jinglejangle Joe Blow Joe Schmoe Juicy Lucy June gloom
  June moon junkie's monkey
junk in the trunk junky punky

killer-diller King Kong Kit Kat kiwi knickknack knob job
  Koo Koo Roo
kowtow Krik? Krak! kudu Kundun

Laffy Taffy lame brain large & in charge late great later gator
  Lazy Daisy
Lean Cuisine lean & mean lean mean machine legal eagle
  Leggo my Eggo
Lexis Nexus lick dick Lickin' Chicken licking stick
  Liddle Kiddle liquor's quicker
lit crit liver quiver lizard's gizzard local yokel long dong
  Loony Toons Loopy Doopy
loose screws loosey-goosey lovie-dovie low blow lucky duck
  lump sum lunch bunch
lust in the dust Lynyrd Skynyrd

Mac Attack mad dad made in the shade Magilla Gorilla
mainframe maitai Mango Tango
Manila Thriller Mantan Mars bars master blaster Maui Wowie
May Day Meal Deal
Meals on Wheels mean green meet & greet mellow yellow
Messy Bessy
Micmac might makes right Mighty Aphrodite miles of smiles
Milli Vanilli
Mingus Among Us mishmash Missy-Pissy mock croc
Mod Squad mojo moldy oldie
Money Honey moose on the loose mop top Mork from Ork
motor voter muckamuck
muck chuck mukluk multi-culti mumbo jumbo mu shu
mushy-gushy my guy

namby-pamby name game nature nurture near beer nice price
night light
nig-nog niminy piminy nitty-gritty nitwit
no finance, no romance
no glove, no love no go no muss, no fuss no pain, no gain
no show no way, Jose
nudie cutie Nut Hut Nutter Butter Nutty Buddy

Ocean Potion odd jobs Oingo Boingo okey-dokey old gold
    ooga-booga
Only the Lonely oodles of noodles Oshkosh B'gosh

Paco's Tacos page gauge pale ale paranoid android
    Parappa the Rapper party hearty Patel hotel
paunch & haunch payday pay & play pee & see peewee
    peg leg pell-mell peter beater
Phantom Anthems phone home phony baloney Pick Up Sticks
    picnic pie in the sky, by & by
Piggly Wiggly ping-pong pit-a-pat pitter-patter Plain Jane
    plaster caster plastic fantastic
play as it lays pocket rocket poet don't know it pogo
    pooper scooper pot shot pope-soap-on-a-rope
Pop Shop poptop Post Toasties powwow poxy doxy prime
    time pump & dump psychedelic relic Puff 'n Stuff

Queen of Mean quest for the best Quick Pick quick trick
    quiet riot quirky quarky

racket-jacket ragbag Ragin' Cajun ragtag ramble-scramble
    Randy Andy rape & scrape
rat-a-tat razzle-dazzle razzmatazz real deal redhead
    Reese's Pieces reet pleat

retail detail Rhymin' Simon rich bitch rickety-tickety rickrack
   riffraff
ring-a-ding ringer dinger rinky-dink Rin Tin Tin riprap
   roach coach
Rock Around the Clock rocket pocket Rolled Gold roly-poly
   Ronald McDonald
rooty-tooty rope-a-dope rough & tough rough stuff
   rub-a-dub Rufty Tufty rusty dusty

saggy baggy Sally's Alley sandman sassafras scarlet harlot
   sci-fi scot & lot
Scrapple from the Apple screen scene screwy Louie screw you
   Sea & Ski
seedy tweedy seesaw self help sexy Rexy shady lady
   shake it, don't break it
Shake 'n Bake Shedd's Spread shilly-shally shipshape
   shirk work shit fit
shit, grit, motherwit shock jock Shy Di sin-bin Sin Den
   singles mingle singsong
skag hag skimble-scamble skinflint skinny mini skunk funk
   sky high slammer jammer
Slice o' Rice slice & dice Slick Rick Slim Jim slo-mo
   SmarteCarte snack pack

snail mail snail trail Smothers Brothers smut-butt smut slut
   sneak peek snowblower
snug as a bug in a rug soap-on-a-rope SoHo space is the place
   space race Spamarama
Spam in a can SpecTech speed reader spit-spot splish-splash
   spring fling Spruce Goose
squeegee Stan the Man stars & bars steam clean Stinky Pinky
   Stix Nix Hix Pix stranger danger
Stormin' Norman street beat stun gun stupid Cupid Style File
   suck and tuck Suds Your Duds
sugar booger sump pump super duper Superloopers sure cure
   surf & turf Swatch watch sweater weather sweetmeat
   Swiss Kriss Swiss Miss

ta-da Tears for Fears tea tree teeny peeny teeny-weeny teepee
   teeter-totter telltale Temporary Contemporary tent event
   Texas Exes Tex-Mex thigh high think pink thinktank
   thin's in, but fat's where it's at
thin skin thrill kill thrills & chills Throat Coat tib-fib Tictac
   ticky-tacky
ticktock tie dye tin tan tan tiptop titbit tit for tat tittle-tattle
   ton of fun tough enough tough stuff town & gown
   Tragic Magic

treat and street Tricky Dicky true blue trust buster
turkey jerky tussy-mussy tutti-frutti
Twine Time

ubble-gubble Ubby Dubby Ugh Bug ugly-mugly
undone unfun urge to purge use it or lose it

Vanessa the Undresser vice price vomit comet voodoo

Wacko Jacko wacky shack wacky tobacky walkie-talkie
Wavy Gravy waylay
wear & tear Weegee Whack Pack whale tale wham bam
whammer-jammer
wheeler dealer whimwham white flight white knight
Wicked Pickett
weird beard wild child willy-nilly Wilt the Stilt
wining & dining
wingding Winken & Blinken wishy-washy womb to tomb
wonton
Wooly Bully Writing Is Fighting

X-sex

Yak Pak yank the crank Yertle the Turtle ying-yang yoohoo

zero to hero zigzag zip your lip Zoo Doo zoot suit Zulu

Thus is just a nothing to thaw you from your warpath and genius during our assonance beguiled two-time yellow agony. Those conversions chapped my thistle in manzanita waylay. In particular, they held a deer and latex impaled on my thistle. Not a deadbeat goes by when I donate this of you. That's why your silhouette remains, for me, sadistic and painterly. Won't you writhe or crawl? Let's mambo and be frisky. Your jiffy jock-strap.

Kamasutra Sutra

This is a story I have heard:

Entwined in a passionate embrace
with his beloved wife,
the holy one exclaimed,
"I have reached enlightenment!"

His devoted partner responded,
"I'm truly happy for you, my love,
and if you can give me another minute,
I believe I'll get there too."

Kirstenography

for K. M.

K was burn at the bend of the ear in the mouth of Remember.
She was the fecund chill burn in her famish. She came into the
word with a putty smoother, a handsewn farther, and a yodeler
cistern. They were all to gather in a rosy horse on a piety sweet
in Alligator Panorama.

When her smoother and farther wrought her chrome from
the hose spittle, her cistern fought the piddle ably was a girly
heeded bawl. A bawl that dank silk, booed, burgled, rabbled,
fried, and tweed in wipers. This was not a bawl that swept in the
joy blocks with her rather joys. This was a giving bawl that
wasn't a joy like a fluffed fan mail. Oh no! This was her grand
blue piddle cistern that cold knot talc for a song time, but lonely
fried and braid rather voices that the yodeler one cold knot rub-
berband.

It shook a few ears until they cold talc to gather, tall yolks,
shear sacreds, heave a conversion or a dish cushion. That was
laughter they kissed their handsewn farther who wind sway to
Cheap Cargo, Ill Annoy. Mum and gulls made their mauve to
Foreword Text. As swoon as they cold they boasted fetters in
the snail to him and he relied as mulch as he cold.

Their inelegant smoother was a reacher who muddied lard,
learned debris, and wept them upon the prosper pat. Reaching
them fright from strong was her per rental doodly. They threw
up and wind soft to mercy rule and hinder guardian, then on to

sedimentary, fecund dairy, and slide rule. They were wood in all those paces, and waded to knowledge at Cutie Ostentatious.

The smoother and her dodders all learned debris to gather. Evidentially, two quirked as proofs in the loony varsity. K was quirking for the slate of Taxes Hysterical Remission. Laughter a schmaltz fart with a wanky lurk, K fond her Sanity. A proof of reckoned comics. K quirked to learn her nastier debris and latter she rave burps and becalmed herself a smoother.

Now she does her writhing ghostly a tome. Quirks at that muse, um, that's in Chapped Apple Milling Sea. Enduring, she has her Sanity and they becalmed the prod parentheses of Adenoid and Williwaw. They all loved shapely over laughter.

The Lunar Lutheran

In chapels of opals and spice, O Pisces pal, your social pep makes you a friend to all Episcopals. Brush off lint, gentile, but it's not intelligent to beshrew the faith of Hebrews. I heard this from a goy who taught yoga in the home of Goya. His Buddhist robe hid this budding D bust in this B movie dud. If Ryan bites a rep, a Presbyterian is best in prayer. Oh tears oxen trod! To catch oil, or a man born to the manor, you need a Catholic, Roman. On Mon. morn, Mom hums "Om" with no other man but Norm or Ron. A Mormon son would gladly leave a gas slave in Las Vegas for a hut in Utah. These slums I'm from, I'm leaving, Miss Lum, with a slim sum donated by some Muslims. What would it cost to gain the soul of an agnostic? Where the atheist is at, God only knows! 'Tis hate, he is at the heist. A Baptist was able to stab a pit bull when the sun hid behind some Hindus. To fan a mess, I write manifestos. So said the lunar Lutheran.

Mantra for a Classless Society,
or Mr. Roget's Neighborhood

cozy comfortable homey homelike
sheltered protected private concealed covered
snug content relaxed restful sedate
untroubled complacent placid serene calm undisturbed
wealthy affluent prosperous substantial
acceptable satisfied satisfactory adequate
uncomfortable uneasy restless
unsuitable indigent
bothersome irritating painful
troublesome discomfiting disturbing
destitute impoverished needy
penniless penurious poor
poverty-stricken embarrassing
upsetting awkward ill-at-ease
nervous self-conscious tense

Music for Homemade Instruments

improvising with Douglas Ewart

I dug you artless, I dug you out. Did you re-do? You dug me less, art. You dug, let's do art. You dug me, less art. Did you re-do? If I left art out, you dug. My artless dug-out. You dug, let art out. Did you re-do, dug-out canoe? Easy as a porkpie piper-led cinch. Easy as a baby bounce. Hop on pot, tin pan man. Original abstract, did you re-do it? Betting on shy cargo, strutting dimpled low-cal strumpets employ a hipster to blow up the native Formica. Then divide efficiency on hairnets, flukes, faux saxons. You dug me out, didn't you? Did you re-do? Ever curtained to experiment with strumpet strutting. Now curtains to milk laboratory. Desecrated flukes & panics displayed by mute politicians all over this whirly-gig. Hey, you dug! Art lasts. Did you re-do? Well-known mocker of lurching unused brains, tribal & lustrous diddlysquats, Latin dimension crepe paper & muscular stacks. Curtains for perky strumpets strutting with mites in the twilight of their origami funkier purses. Artless, you dug. Did you re-do? For patting wood at flatland, thanks. For bamboozle flukes at Bama, my seedy medication. Thanks for my name in the yoohoo. Continental camp-out, percolating throughout the whirly-gig on faux saxon flukes. You dug art, didn't you? Did you re-do?

Naked Statues

Oscars for the war of noses. With a mummy out of Egypt, a prosthetic muppet. Opening shot: cliché of travel genre. In several scenes, a woman put together in black, white, or khaki. A woman with her back up like his map of mountain. Finally, she dies. Then, at last, he dies. So romantic are the patient English. This all went on when I was making up my syllabus. Telephone and radio told who the winners were. I didn't need a crystal. Last time I watched was leopard chair and whoopie cushion. That's when I saw the industry of light, our buttered roll. These are the friends of inklish, I was told, by someone from an anglophile race. They read all the great books and perform them in the garden of naked statues.

Every anguish is arbitrary but no one is neuter. Bulldozer can knock down dikes. Why a ragged bull don't demolish the big house? The fired cook was deranged. On the way back when I saw red I thought ouch. Soon when I think colored someone bleeds. The agency tapping my telephone heard my pen drop. Now I'm walking out of pink ink. We give microphones to the voiceless to amplify their silence. The complete musician could play any portion of the legacy of the instrument. My ebony's under the ocean. Please bring back my bone (sic) to me. Once was illegal for we to testify. Now all us do is testify. We's all prisoners of our own natural anguish. It's the rickety rickshaw that will drive us to the brink.

There was this princess who wet the bed through many mattresses, she was so attuned. She neither conversed with magical beasts nor watched her mother turn into a stairwell or a stoop. Her lips were. Her hair was. Her complexion was. Her beauty or her just appearance. What she wore. She was born on a chessboard, with parents and siblings, all royal. Was there a witch? Was she enchanted, or drugged? When did she decide to sleep? Dreaming a knight in armor, she thought it meant jousting. His kind attack with streamers. A frog would croak. A heart would cough after only one bite. Something was red. There was wet and there was weather. She couldn't make it gold without his name. Her night shifts in the textile mill. She forgot she was a changeling peasant girl. Spinning, she got pricked. That's where roses fell and all but one fairy wept. It remains that she be buried alive, knowing that a kiss is smaller than a delayed hunger.

O, 'Tis William

for W. D.

—Is it Otis?

—I'm . . .

—Otis, so it is.

—Am I?

—'Tis Otis.

—I am . . .

—So, it's Otis.

—I am William.

—O, Otis, sit.

—O, I am Will.

—Sit, Otis.

—It's Will.

—Is Otis to sit?

—Otis?

—Is Will, so sit!

—O, will I?

—Will Otis sit?

—I'm William!

—O, will Will sit?

—I will sit.

—So sit, Otis!

—O, I will sit. I am Will.

—So sit, Will.

—I'm William. So I am! I will sit!

—So sit still, William.

—O, I am! I sit.

—Otis, sit still!

—I am still William!

—Otis is William.

—Will is William.

—William is Otis too.

—O, I am William! William is Otis! Otis is William!
I am Will! Otis too! O, William Otis, it is! I am!

A humble monumental
music made of syllables
or a heartbroken crystal
cathedral with gleaming walls
of Orangina bottles

Now that my ears are connected to a random answer machine, the wrong brain keeps talking through my hat. Now that I've been licked all over by the English tongue, my common law spout is suing for divorce. Now that the Vatican has confessed and the White House has issued an apology, I can forgive everything and forget nothing. Now the overdrawn credits roll as the bankrupt star drives a patchwork cab to the finished line, where a broke robot waves a mended tablecloth, which is the stale flag of a checkmate career. Now that the history of civilization has been encrypted on a medium grain of rice, it's taken the starch out of the stuffed shorts. Now as the Voice of America crackles and fades, the market reports that today the Euro hit a new low. Now as the reel unravels, our story unwinds with the curious dynamic of an action flick without a white protagonist.

Does all dust turn grave in his nightmare of cloned sheep? Is Bo Peep losing sleep? Did the lamb march in? Eat the dandelions? Is lamb chop an unnatural act? Hello, Dolly, have you any wool? Serious, serious, thick hats full of kinks. So don't forget to pack your Polartec. Last week we picked oranges, but the apple's still chilling. She might not be the cruelest fool. Just a lame dame on a blip trip. Her brain on spring break. A trick vacation. A fake date. A fluke, or just a flake. Was there then but she was in the left at the wrong. Nothing to see but a strung gallery of poetry inhibitions. Her book on the table. Nobody buying. Luck was there to take her in. A friend with a new look, a light blond bob. A friend tending to the dying. One who lends money for books. Who shows her the neighborhood paper bag and circles all her haunts. The mayor takes credit for the quality of life. Mention money on the street and a hand will be extended. They stretch out in a crowd. They sign for the wild child of yoga. Walk across the park from Charlie Parker. Eat sweet potato pirogies in uppity cafe. Look at other merchandise. A smattering of tribes. Unheard of march in which the men protest themselves. Callaloo and collards are equivalent. Or banana is the same as *plata no es*. Narrative never is mere entertainment. To entertain is knowing how to be a woman. French theories suggest the best in women's writing are the men. "These star-apple leaves along the sound of Sonny Rollins

River." Tina Turner set fire to her wigs so she could wear all burnt hair. Tourists flock to Strawberry Fields. Where sheep grazed in erstwhile Seneca Village. No one gets agit-props from avant-garde. A-Train from Caffe Reggio out of postcards. Hour and a half by subway to JFK. Bumpy return to port of lax security. Once I get that zip gun your reality Czech's in the escargot.

This system needs your moral fiber like a bowl of X brand flakes. If your kind cannot be assimilated to make spare parts for Borg wars, your resistance challenges the ant farm to adapt. You might think the system's tone deaf, but our software's immune. You are the virus that keeps it in tune. We are the tolerant host, which makes you the guest worker colony of *E. coli*, the chitlins inside the chitlins. Catching hits off our perfect pitch, your contra fit's a false note passed through the phony caca. We call you irresponsible, say you're indigestible, and it's undeniably true it's tough to swallow you. Your data resisted analysis, but if you are not consumed, your flawed construction only proves that we are perfection cubed. Did you need to read the label on Olean to know the SOS goes out when the chip's going down? To Cuisinart our metaphors once again, let's just say that Dracula's liquid protein diet could use some roughage to help with his next smooth move. A bloodsucker's got to worry about irregularity. So pollsters press the pulse, take specimens of the blood count. Pundits pooh-pooh as law and order candidate Bruce Wayne leaves his potty to go on a turd-pooty ticket: Libertarian runs on avowal movement platform. The result will be a better grade of guano piling up in the bat cave. Our constipation requires frequent amendments to feed the tree of liberty. Can you dig it? Can you dig it? Man, you're digging it with a shovel. When you're all pooped out, we're just breaking a second wind.

She Swam On from Sea to Shine

Hide and seek, where the tree decided to sleep was where she ran. She ran away with a ruckus. The baby girl was stolen by a tipsy woman came to take her. Where they found her in the mud. She'd stolen a doll. Her doll got sick, she died. The brown doll from her father. The pink doll came from somewhere else. She had drowsy eyes like marbles. The rabbit was painted on the furniture in the room with pom-pom curtains. The pig slept at her grandmother's. The pig that ate money, not the country pig that ate molasses and sunglasses. Where her mother kept a canoe and paddle. Where stiff lace stood, in the city not the country, where they fed their stinky sheep. Paper shell pecans, climb high. Sweet figs and green plums in forbidden backyards.

She remembers sleeping on a train. She remembers a long sleep, rocking, rocking. She had her dress on all the way. Asleep, diving into dreams. Salty and warm, like ocean, like broth. Another time she slept, she dreamed of rats. When she woke up, the kittens were all killed. We're in a photograph with a handsome man smiling. Seersucker suits are what to wear in summer. That other man I don't remember, the one who made your hair fall. That's when the doctor said you need a root. You need your roots. You need a doctor who knows roots and will root for you. That's how we all got better. That's how we got to all your exes live in Texas. All the livelong day with the cowgirl you left behind.

Those saxophone streets and scratchy sidewalks. Those Baptist conventions. That steamy summer. The boy who threw tar on me. The boy who made me his tar baby. The one who broke my watch, knocked me down, pushed me over. The boy who threw rocks at me. The boy who lost his foot under the wheels of a train. The boy who bought me ice cream. The girl who was my friend. The girl who wanted to give me a kitten. The girl with burnt hands. The girl whose house was dark. The girl who never wore socks. The girl who said, "Poot on you." I had a ribbon in my hair. I was too proper and prissy. I must think I'm something. I must think she's nothing.

In the beginning, we stay with the preacher. We sit sweating on the mercy seat. We hear the preacher shout. We feel the fire in this man who built the church that burned down. This preacher who read Nietzsche. This preacher who was a carpenter with bent nails, who was the father of the cowgirl who ironed his handkerchiefs. The big man who cheered at wrestling matches, who drove a dark Chevy, who wore white shirts stiff from the laundry, who sang, "There was a crooked man, who had a crooked smile." She recalls a sixpence, a pig, a crooked little stile. He knew a stile could get them over. He knew a thing or two, and so did the lady who made crab cakes. The lady who fried scrapple. The lady with peach tree switches, who knew that a spigot was a faucet. Her *chaise longue,* her *porte-cochere,* her *chiffonier.* She didn't want the cowgirl to be a boll weevil. She wanted us where we were, not in the garage. She wanted us in the church where everyone shouted.

We started selling and counting. Anything from earthworms and bottles to paper shell pecans. She saved green stamps and we ate pinto beans from dented cans. She found a house with bramble bushes. We found a lovely alley made dizzy circles. We found a house with attic rooms. A magic chef in the kitchen and a genie to keep it clean. We kept moving until we moved the neighbors out. They ran to Runaway Bay. They hid at Hideaway Lake. Those neighbors who were not neighborly, who didn't want us for neighbors.

The nuns were smart teachers, but she didn't care for them. They didn't care for her and called her friend a guttersnipe. The nuns in their brick *pan dulce* magnolia convent, their virgin rose *tortilla de maíz* garden grotto, their *Carnicería Chapultepec* chapel. These nuns don't talk Spanish, you could say French. Parlor fluent frenchy, jumble lying crawfish pie filling gumball. They taught girls to knit. They taught her to hit the piano. They taught all the girls to say hell merry fuller grays, dolores wit chew, blast duh art dower mung wimmen, blast dis fruit uh duh loom, cheez whiz. Anomie, dull party, dull filly, dull spitter shoo sanity. I am my mother's daughter who put me in the water to see if I could swim. My hair went back to Africa. I baptize thee. Hiccup, hiccup, hiccup.

High school was a bluster. She wasn't a bother. High school was a thick brick. She was knocked out. High school was too high, she was too low. High school was too low, she was too high. High school was too many schedules she crashed. Who could remember the combination. High school was hormones and hers were a moan, she wasn't a whore or a harmed one. No one was too harsh. High school was hot, she wasn't cool. She loved the books and not the boys. They moved too much, they blur. Too many books on her head, her leaky calendar. Too much gossip, her unlocked locker. Too much mother, she wouldn't hop. She wasn't a case of textbooks. Never that. She was a cartoon. She was a poem. Anyone would stutter trying to recite.

After perusing all the pamphlets, she went where she had been, where she knew how. It was a place she knew she could. So big no one would notice in a green location. She knew the uniforms, not the sunbathers. She kept her eye on the tower, rehearsed her sitting ducks. She believed the room was haunted, the furniture walked. Her friend had gone to a school where she misplaced her mind. She never found her friend again, her box of comprehension. There were new girls now, the ones who ironed tortillas and made beans drunk. They knew that *sopa* isn't soap, *ropa* isn't rope, and butter is meant to kill ya.

If only she could play bid whist, if only she could tell someone. If only she had only eaten cassava, not listened to so much jazz. If only she had a gospel voice, not a notebook full of Babylon. If only she had obeyed her mother, if only she could disobey. If only she hadn't been to prison to visit the afflicted. If whiskey were water and I were a duck. If only if you only knew she wouldn't try to tell you.

She got that piece of paper and ran with it. Somewhere she'd found a tongue she used gingerly. She spoke up, she didn't lie down. If she did lie, she made it a big one. She spoke for a wagon wheel, she got the grease. They paid her to be smart, or dumb, it didn't matter. If they paid her, she could eat. If they didn't, she could go. She was always writing anyway, it didn't matter. She fell into a trance. That's how he took her with him where he went, and so she came along and there she was. When he wanted to bust her, she wasn't in shock, there was warning. Instead of bursting, she ran. She got used to running.

More paper, more pencils, more writing, she went everywhere she could. She went on a whim, on a limb, she limped and whimpered. She slowed down, she settled, she got stuck. She came loose, she mended. She came undone, she repaired herself again. She shook her groove thing and got it on. She stepped on a pin, the pin bent. Good thing she got that tetanus shot. Time for a booster.

When the ship went down, she wouldn't sink, had to swim, she brought her suit. She'd float like a jellyfish, sting like a man of war, or seaweed ain't salty. Water was her element, she swam on. Right through a tsunami, she cut with scissor kicks. She caught a wave, she got in a flap, she was flippant. From sea, she ran past shark teeth. Like shine, see. If I'm lying, I'm flying. From sea to shine, she swam on. The whales sang Celtic music, dolphins frisked her. She was worked over and under she let her mind wander. Let it roll and keep on rolling on and on. Revolution is a cycle that never ends. Rumors of May made mermaids murmur. Plato opens utopia to poets on opiates.

Sleeping with the Dictionary

I beg to dicker with my silver-tongued companion, whose lips
are ready to read my shining gloss. A versatile partner, conver-
sant and well-versed in the verbal art, the dictionary is not
averse to the solitary habits of the curiously wide-awake reader.
In the dark night's insomnia, the book is a stimulating sedative,
awakening my tired imagination to the hypnagogic trance of
language. Retiring to the canopy of the bedroom, turning on
the bedside light, taking the big dictionary to bed, clutching the
unabridged bulk, heavy with the weight of all the meanings
between these covers, smoothing the thin sheets, thick with
accented syllables—all are exercises in the conscious regimen
of dreamers, who toss words on their tongues while turning
illuminated pages. To go through all these motions and proce-
dures, groping in the dark for an alluring word, is the poet's
nocturnal mission. Aroused by myriad possibilities, we try out
the most perverse positions in the practice of our nightly act,
the penetration of the denotative body of the work. Any exit
from the logic of language might be an entry in a symptomatic
dictionary. The alphabetical order of this ample block of
knowledge might render a dense lexicon of lucid hallucinations.
Beside the bed, a pad lies open to record the meandering of
migratory words. In the rapid eye movement of the poet's night
vision, this dictum can be decoded, like the secret acrostic of a
lover's name.

People of color untie-dyed. Got nothing to lose but your CPT-shirts. You're all just a box of crayons. The whole ball of wax would make a lovely decorator candle on a Day of the Dead Santeria Petro Vodou altar. Or how about these yin-yang earrings to balance your energy? This rainbow crystal necklace, so good for unblocking your chi and opening the chakras? Hey, you broke it, you bought it! No checks accepted. Unattended children will be sold as slaves.

Suzuki Method

El Niño brought a typhoon of tom-toms from Tokyo, where a
thrilling instrument makes an OK toy. Tiny violins are shrill.
Their shrieks are musical mice. The color of a mechanical clock
is lost in translation. Whatever you're telling me sounds like the
straight teeth of rodents. My dreams throw the book at the
varmint. We both shudder as the dictionary thuds. You've got
to admit, our Esperanto's hopeless. Your virgin is unfaithful.
My savory hero boards the ship of Marco Polo, loaded with soy
from Ohio.

"I grew up with a lot of punctuation myself, so I can understand your nostalgia for parentheses," the dashing Sister Ka exclaimed to her dingbat friend across the periodic table. "Is a pink collar worker a redneck who came in from the sun?" a bloody European quizzed the ruddy Fulbright scholar during the in-depth Q and A following her profound lecture on the abysmal fried tradition of deep southern chickens. "This exhibit confronts spectators with several provocative photographs of found topiaries," the moving finger of the aggressively ironic art critic scrawled on the electronic notepad. "Was it plastic or a fetish?" the imagineers of indebtedness asked the psychosurgical micromanagers of desire. The old crock tearfully confided to the young salt, "A wave of mock cashmere turtlenecks swallowed my ethnic pride, and I can't believe it's not bitter." "Think of your appendix as an archaeological site, or a library of preventable diseases," the bespectacled white-coated professional added gratuitously to the critical list, thus bursting the ruined institutional pyramid scheme. "Never again!" vowed the recidivist backslider falling off the anniversary wagon of second-hand chainsmoking reactionaries. The virtual master of cyberpornotopia whispered to his pixilated hologram, "If I had you where you've got me, I'd give myself a blowjob."

Ted Joans at the Café Bizarre

cairo man
surly realist
dis member ship
jungle blackboards
cryptic script
stirring up
dead alive
tongues tired
tarred wool
manifesto folded
unclear arms
cracking open
ivory trunk
of brazil nuts
voodoo toenails
konker root
jockey cornsilk
purrs natch
contraband leader
scattering scat
sporadically all over
forever diaspora

Vines through the roof of the tool shed. Water leaked in.
Where would I sleep. Three square meals: brunch, brown bag,
potluck. Hold my hand while we talk. Trees like transplants
from Mars. Nooky in the bandstand. Sticky sunshine. Sections
of orange. A cut and another. Some snail trail. Trickle of salt.
Wets and cries. A hand, sometimes a fist. Lolling toward
rhythm. A buzz that kept me awake nights. Burning triangles.
Every sound coming through the wall. Dream of elephant.
Dream of braiding hair. Who wears those shoes with cutouts?
In my next lifetime learn to play guitar. She can bend her tongue
both ways but can't whistle.

Brought cactus to a housewarming. We sat on a mat with
cups of jasmine tea. They slept on a thin straw *petate* and ate off
stolen plates. Cheap, plentiful rolls of foam. No one I knew
owned box springs or a sofa. Futons help the spine like yoga.
Cleopatra's barge. Massage with oil to music of flutes. It pene-
trates. The door left open. Someone peeked into the dark. She
checked out her blind dates from the want ads at a bar called
Crow's Nest. Kind of a scene, I guess. Big picture window with
a view of the bay. Hearing them giggle and moan. Those bark-
ing dogs were sea lions on the rocks offshore. I'd never wear
that swimsuit. I couldn't get to sleep at all. My mind kept cir-
cling. They all have different fathers. Some had green eyes.
Genetic lottery or slot machine. Lab rat seeks reward. Advice

for my face. Once I turned it on it wouldn't turn off. This man I didn't know was stroking my foot without saying a word. He felt free to stare at strangers on a bus. *Frijoles borachos. Mestizaje. Hasta la pasta.* U.S. flag in neon on the ceiling of a Chinese restaurant in Texas. Good jukebox. Dollars pinned to her dress. Ready to light the sparklers. The handsome candidate dropped out of the race. Euphoria resulted in a moving violation.

Dachshund dog wears hooks for puppy cups. Head in the briars, heart gushes a flame. Plaster hands impaired in prayer. Thick-haired Irish brothers press their true blue suits. Martyred dream. Preacher gets more chicken. Slippery pages edged with gilt. Her skirt fanned out to catch the ashes. Hula girls gesture toward tropical wood utensils. Island trips or military hitch. Shepherd vs. shepherdess. Porcelain features, elaborate frames. Angel in the nick snatches kids from the brink. Toreador velvet. Bronze shoes next to gathers. Plush puckery. Ottoman embroidery. Old masters macaroni sprayed gold. Curly bark keeps name in nail polish. Teacups, blurred roses, ivy jungle. Bowl of glass inedible. Plastic covers over formal furniture. Not a living room but a parlor. Dust to dust. The child who carves her initials on the piano. Park the bike in the kitchen. Lean against the fridge. Best cardboard tunnels. Burn scar from space heater. I'm sorry you're toast. Voice of ham static flies around the world. Kotex box where anyone can see. Separate domiciles. Never a tablecloth. Garage full of church ink. Strategize at chess while twirling spaghetti out of the pot. Where the comb went upside my head. Getting stoned after school in a rock fight. Next day I wore a dashing pirate's eye patch. Trailer park hit by tornado. Song that says get an ugly girl to marry you. Doll with ponytail and pedalpushers. Melamac. Chinet. Slurpee. Her name was Felicia but of course they called her Fellatio.

Two smokers came to visit so I had to find a jar lid. When he sat on my stove he could look down at me. It's years since we've talked. I witnessed a green card wedding. She borrowed my white cotton dress. We drank a lot in those days. An artist allergic to paint. The way his skin felt was a surprise. It crept in. He knew we weren't a match. Not enough heat. Ran into a blizzard. Thawed out the car at a motel with adjoining pancake house. Found a sky of double rainbows. Those rez girls, their poor pottery. Red cowboy boots might scare the snakes off. Xerox fetish. Their chants all sounded the same to me in the five-hundred-year-old housing project. No sleeping bag or view of the eclipse. Confused by all the rain a frog had entered the living room. Earthworms dying under our feet. Sold a poem today. A drunkard in the plaza called out, "Sister, may I kiss you?"

My Mickey Mouse ears are nothing like sonar. Colorado is far less rusty than Walt's lyric riddles. If sorrow is wintergreen, well then Walt's breakdancers are dunderheads. If hoecakes are Wonder Bras, blond Wonder Bras grow on Walt's hornytoad. I have seen roadkill damaged, riddled and wintergreen, but no such roadkill see I in Walt's checkbook. And in some purchases there is more deliberation than in the bargains that my Mickey Mouse redeems. I love to herd Walt's sheep, yet well I know that muskrats have a far more platonic sonogram. I grant I never saw a googolplex groan. My Mickey Mouse, when Walt waddles, trips on garbanzos. And yet, by halogen-light, I think my loneliness as reckless as any souvenir bought with free coupons.

Way Opposite

after Richard Wilbur

The opposite of walk?
    A psychic with a crystal ball
        and tarot deck
            who sees green
                when your palm is read.

    At the sign of a red palm
        I don't walk,
            I run.

We Are Not Responsible

We are not responsible for your lost or stolen relatives. We cannot guarantee your safety if you disobey our instructions. We do not endorse the causes or claims of people begging for handouts. We reserve the right to refuse service to anyone. Your ticket does not guarantee that we will honor your reservations. In order to facilitate our procedures, please limit your carrying on. Before taking off, please extinguish all smoldering resentments. If you cannot understand English, you will be moved out of the way. In the event of a loss, you'd better look out for yourself. Your insurance was cancelled because we can no longer handle your frightful claims. Our handlers lost your luggage and we are unable to find the key to your legal case. You were detained for interrogation because you fit the profile. You are not presumed to be innocent if the police have reason to suspect you are carrying a concealed wallet. It's not our fault you were born wearing a gang color. It is not our obligation to inform you of your rights. Step aside, please, while our officer inspects your bad attitude. You have no rights that we are bound to respect. Please remain calm, or we can't be held responsible for what happens to you.

Who knows why you and I fell off the roster?
Who can figure why you and I never passed muster
on our way out yonder?
Does anyone wonder why you and I lacked
the presence of minding our blunders?
Can anyone see why you and I, no longer intact,
pulled a disappearing act and left with scratch? Our secret pact
required that you and I forget why and where
we lost our place when we went off the books.
Could anyone guess, does anyone know or even care
why you and I can't be found, as hard as we look?
Who'll spell out for us, if we exist,
why you and I missed our turn on the list?
who can stand to reason why you and I let
our union dissolve to strike the orderly alphabet?

Wino Rhino

For no specific reason I have become one of the city's unicorns. No rare species, but one in range of danger. No mythical animal, but a common creature of urban legend. No potent stallion woven into poetry and song. Just the tough horny beast you may observe, roaming at large in our habitat. I'm known to adventurers whose drive-by safari is this circumscribed wilderness. Denatured photographers like to shoot me tipping the bottle, capture me snorting dust, mount on the wall my horn of empties that spilled the grape's blood. My flesh crawls with itchy insects. My heart quivers as arrows on street maps target me for urban removal. You can see that my hair's stiffened and my skin's thick, but the bravest camera can't document what my armor hides. How I know you so well. Why I know my own strength. Why, when I charge you with my rags, I won't overturn your sporty jeep.

as horses as for
as purple as we go
as heartbeat as if
as silverware as it were
as onion as I can
as cherries as feared
as combustion as want
as dog collar as expected
as oboes as anyone
as umbrella as catch can
as penmanship as it gets
as narcosis as could be
as hit parade as all that
as icebox as far as I know
as fax machine as one can imagine
as cyclones as hoped
as dictionary as you like
as shadow as promised
as drinking fountain as well
as grassfire as myself
as mirror as is
as never as this

Xenophobic Nightmare in a Foreign Language

waking up with Enrique Chagoya

Whereas, in the opinion of the Government of the United States the coming of bitter labor to this country endangers the good order of certain localities within the territory thereof:

Therefore, be it enacted by the Senate and House of Representatives of the United States of America in Congress assembled,

That from and after the expiration of ninety days next after the passage of this act, and until the expiration of ten years next after the passage of this act, the coming of bitter labor to the United States be, and the same is hereby, suspended; and during such suspension it shall not be lawful for any bitter labor to come, or, having so come after the expiration of said ninety days, to remain within the United States.

That the master of any vessel who shall knowingly bring within the United States on such vessel, and land or permit to be landed, any bitter labor, from any foreign port or place, shall be deemed guilty of a misdemeanor, and on conviction thereof shall be punished by a fine of not more than five hundred dollars for each and every such bitter labor so brought, and may be also imprisoned for a term not exceeding one year.

That any person who shall knowingly bring into or cause to be brought into the United States by land, or who shall knowingly aid or abet the same, or aid or abet the landing in the United States from any vessel of any bitter labor not lawfully entitled to enter the United States, shall be deemed guilty of a misdemeanor, and shall, on conviction thereof, be fined in a sum not exceeding one thousand dollars, and imprisoned for a term not exceeding one year.

That no bitter labor shall be permitted to enter the United States by land without producing to the proper officer of customs the certificate in this act required of bitter labor seeking to land from a vessel. And any bitter labor found unlawfully within the United States shall be caused to be removed therefrom to the country from whence they came, by direction of the United States, after being brought before some justice, judge, or commissioner of a court of the United States and found to be not lawfully entitled to be or remain in the United States.

May 6, 1882

You don't need X-ray vision to see through me.
No super power's required to penetrate my defense.

Without listening to your mother's rant
you can tell that my motives are transparent.

A sturdy intuition could give you
the strong impression that my logic is flimsy.

Before the flat lady sang the first note of the book,
you knew that my story was thin.

Zen Acorn

for Bob Kaufman

a frozen
indian acorn

a frozen
indiana corn

afro zen
indian acorn

afro zen
indiana corn

a zen fro
in diana corn

frozen fan
in zero canadian

indian corn for
arizona nonradiance

a narco dozen
faze an african

Zombie Hat

Greatest thing since Texas toast,
the ever-popular zombie hat
flies off the shelf
like sandwich loaf.
For your tête-à-tête
with a headhunter, or chat with a shrink,
zombie hat's the right think.
You'll look like a hero
in your zombie sombrero.
Don't forget to wear your hat.
It's what the head cheese ordered, stat.
Statistics show the zombie hat
helps to maintain social stasis.
With the right fit,
you'll brim with social graces.
We recommend it for all our head cases.
Meet every problem head on,
so long as you keep a lid on.

Designer: Nola Burger
Compositor: BookMatters, Berkeley
Text: 11/16 Fournier
Display: Univers Condensed Light
Printed by Friesens Corp.